I Never Finished Loving You

By Philip Butera

JaCol Publishing Inc.

FIRST PRINTING

February 2020

JaCol Publishing Inc.
195 Murica Aisle
Irvine, CA 92614
818-510-2898
Editor-in-Chief: Randall
Andrews
www.jacolpublishing.com

ISBN: 978-1-946675-37-8

Acknowledgment

There are moments in the course of writing when the right word appears to follow the correct one. They fall into place and celebrate themselves by having meaning. The message you want to communicate is there, the images you want to convey are clear, and the drama is evident.

At other times, hours pass, days sometimes, maybe a week, and the word you are searching for remains elusive. A writer cannot work without the proper tools, and there are so many proper tools; imagination, creativity, enlightenment, intelligence, originality, aptitude, and most definitely patience. I could go on, and in the end, I would also need to include timing and luck. There needs to be structure, form, cadence, knowledge, and there are hundreds of excellent books, classes, and videos that spell it out for all who want to learn.

What is also needed, though, are family and friends that believe in you and, most importantly, are honest with you. I am fortunate for when the frustrations become monumental, and I want to rip apart the hundreds of books that surround me and everything I have ever written. I look at the titles of those books and realize what they have meant to not just me but others. I walk into another room or make a call. A discussion begins about writing or about art in general, and the question surfaces, "Would you rather be doing anything else?" There is never any doubt, there is nothing I would rather do than explore my mind for the precise word that is needed to express what is in my heart.

I want to thank those in the other rooms and on the phone who have listened, calmed, and encouraged me to fulfill my dreams – to become an author and be known as a poet.

Thank-you: Lauren, Diane, Kathryn, Jay, Dan, Nicole, Joe, Bruce, Lorna, Maxx, Chris, and Sam

Dedicated

To those who have never finished loving someone

Artwork by Alex Alemany
E-Mail: Alex@alexalemany.com
www.alexalemany.com

FOREWARD

"Philip Butera glides, rides, manipulates, caresses, seduces, and inhabits language. While his images and phrasing initially appear complex and constant, he manages to be clear and concise with both. To call him anything short of a verbal genius would be a denial of his unparalleled ownership of the richest of all languages."

Kathleen Bryce Niles, Editor, Comstock Review

"Philip Butera's 'I Never Finished Loving You' is an insightful book of poetry that encompasses emotions deeper than most of us ever dare to delve into. Be prepared to have your eyes opened to a poetic universe where things are not always as they seem. A universe where he questions if poets should pilot skyrockets, and not drive cars. Where love is always right around the next corner, dark thoughts follow your every step, and the mirror is always hiding the truth. Philip's vibrant language and artistic visions will have you clamoring for more."

Ann Christine Tabaka, multi-award-winning poet

"The sheer talent and skill of Philip Butera as a writer simply can not be disputed. He is a language wizard when using the written word to present imagery, ideas, and feelings that are profound yet easily absorbed by the

reader. Additionally, if poetry is meant to be read aloud, Butera's work is satisfying indeed."

Salvatore Alessi, Adjunct Professor of Literature, Canisius College

"Philip Butera uses words and phrases like an accomplished artist uses color and light. Excellent balance of imagery and abstraction. His command of language is broad and lush."

Nicole Washburn, Editor, and Ghostwriter

"Philip's beautifully dangerous poetry captivates the reader with intensely revealing intimacy."

Teresa Ann Frazee – Artist and Poet, Founder of the Boca Museum of Art, Art & Literature Series

"With raw passion and profound psychological perception, Philip's poetry pierces your innermost being."

Eva E. A. Skoe, Ph.D. Professor Emeritus of Psychology

Contents

Under Ice

The gales and the gusts
have no memory of their journeys.

I am lost and forgotten under the ice.
I touch the surface and feel the cold.

Clouds hide the sun,
the moon is milky,
and the harsh winds sweep across breaking waves.

Without you,
I shudder to anticipate
more of winter's long shadow
and what the thaw will bring.

There is no Tracking Reason

I stepped out the door
tiptoeing on clouds,
looking behind stars.
Yearning.
I followed moonbeams,
on a comet.
Dashed across the sun
visiting the planets
even
touched heaven,
longing,
longing.

Holding binoculars
I soared on the wings of a jet,
slid down Everest,
then
rode mules and camels to cross the desert.
I navigated the oceans

watched whales swim freely
spoke to sea birds
and
eased in and out of memories
craving you.

I enjoyed the warmth of the tropics,
ran among the colors of rainbows.
In the arctic
I thought
you are as unforgettable as the northern lights.
I journeyed on the hands of time
wincing from the rain as the winds wailed.

Finally,
a hurricane delivered me to the lonely place I began.
There is no tracking reason,
through my tears, I can still see you
and the taste of you
will linger forever.

When I Fell from Everest

When I fell from Everest,
you said
my tears
did not move you.

I jumped
from
planes and trains.
Flawed, broken
and depressed
I ran to you.

You laughed,
as we watched my blood
follow the curb
to the sewer grates.

You disappeared,
into a bar,

where the heartless
sacrifice the innocent.

I filled a canvas
with thick reds, crimson, and scarlet
pretending our lips had merged.
I saw me through your eyes,
a poem without words.

Perhaps, I may fall once more
but
I will never be helpless again.

When I Thought of you

Once,
when I thought of you,
my phone would ring.
You would gush about the bright yellow sun in an artist's blue sky,
about clouds like white horses galloping,
and you whirling in fields of hyacinths.
We measured time lyrically,
embroidering our hunger for each other
with a curiousness unrestrained.

Once,
posing nude for a painter, you said, "Intimacy is just a new arrangement of curves and lines."
After you found a new lover
I discovered crows had replaced thrushes in the woods we used to explore.

Once,

as I watched the moon

find its place among the stars,

I drew lines to find the constellation

we created,

wondering what did I hope to see.

The Carnival Colossus of Rhodes

Legs from open to closed,
the clanging of the bottles
when you left the bed.
Breasts are back in their caskets.
I could have climbed Mount Olympus
but you blocked the path.
You pushed me aside.

Your car roared away
to arrive somewhere else.
I am frightened by the devil,
who shares my mind.
There is no escape,
knives are available, and guns are loaded.

The carnival Colossus of Rhodes,
legs apart lights the way.
There is the banging in my head,
Hades always has a welcoming brashness.

I live between the mirror and the reflection.
Astonishing images slither through my head,
reverberations of troubles in bondage.
At the edge of my thoughts suicide calls,
she is loud and persistent.
Scissors separate assumption from indifference.
There is no relief, just pounding,
prophetic avalanches push away reasoning.
Illumination crashes into despairing shadows.
The scaffold of my mind collapsing,
yet I think these are not my thoughts.
You took them with you,
leaving behind a frantic jazz beat and an abstract poet's
cynicism.

Is that your car coming back?
If the devil is banished, why do I remain?
I see the headlights.
Love is just running into yourself,
over
and over again;

The mirrors

The witnesses

The relentlessness

the indulgent smiles and looming disappointments.

It is you!

I bury myself in your flesh,

But all that is left are threads of words

spoken but never meant.

Not Caring, I lied

Not caring, I lied.
Nothing lasts for long,
except for heartache
and self-doubt.
I am still tumbling from changes,
still cautious when the light
turns green.

What I said
about searching for meaning
I meant for myself.
All my words are traumatized images,
that I stumble over
never seeing the danger.

Stay close to your ocean waves.
Remain a watercolor dreamer
in search of no words
that display themselves

as life rafts.

The Anchor

"Don't be kind,"

I said, "It would be out of character."

Months after you left me

I boarded a cruise ship.

How lonely slipping out to sea,

a courier on liquid, surrounded by seams

of blues and whites.

Waves unfurl with indifference,

the sun glistens with halos of colored rings.

As you watch the moodiness of the sea, minutes

lengthen.

Once again, I feel the coring of contemplation.

The mind is cruel; it lacks pity for its thoughts.

A petite woman with almond eyes and a slight scar on

her pale cheek offers me a drink.

I order sailors' favorite, dark rum.

We chat about imaginings and romantic fantasies.

As if sleepwalking, I go to her cabin.
She readily offers me her breasts,
a hundred monologues remain on her brown nipples.
She reaches into me,
into an inhospitable heart, empty, with tattered edges.

Now, alone and cold,
briny air in my nostrils, I think of you,
naked and beguiling wanting someone but not me.

A siren calls as an anchor is released,
I watch the cabling curl around my legs,
A loudspeaker sounds an alarm,
whistles stir, nautical language - *Someone Overboard.*
Faces search mirrors to verify their existence.
For a time, the ship circles, and circles.
Hungry seabirds gather in clusters.
The circles become larger until the distance and past are
indistinguishable.
Eventually, serenity prevails.

Stars frame a bright crescent moon.

The woman with the small scar opens her blouse

for the chilly wind to kiss her breasts.

She sighs and drops a white rose into the ocean.

The Weight of Dying Desires

My tears,
cloud the storm.
My arms are wrapped around my legs,
head on knees,
rocking myself.
Holding myself captive.

Again,
another fall.
Waves crash,
motive and judgment collide.
The twilight of love
can be felt at dawn,
as the once morning kiss
is now a glance.
And the petty wounds
become deep cuts
hardening
into scars.

Disillusionment creeps from the mind,

into the flesh,

the weight of dying desires.

Despair,

like a merciless serpent, reveals itself.

Ordinary things with sharp edges become considerations.

And the connection between believing and knowing

is a twirling, twisting barb

delving deeper

into unhappiness.

Room

I want to be in a room with
no windows,
no outside patio,
no escape.

A room with a bed,
a fireplace,
a piano,
and books from floor to ceiling.

I don't want to hear the news.
I don't want to listen to my neighbors.
I don't want to be a part of the madness.

A room where
my imagination
comforts,
and pleases me.

You keep the key to my room.

Slip in at times and lay next to me

I will use simple words rather than emotions

to ask you to stay.

Enjoying the Flight of Dreams

A raven perched on a branch,
she surveyed her surroundings.
It was afternoon,
sunlight with clairvoyant hues captured what my
thoughts,
the ones on the fringe, next to dreams wanted to express.

In a curious way,
I wanted to leave behind images,
this was prominent in the way I placed my easel.
I kept my intellect at bay, always a prospect of danger,
when I confront myself without mindfulness.
I took up my brush,
it scolded me for being precise,
it wanted freedom.

I decided to watch,
I set my desires aside, they immediately gathered
with phantoms of paintings past.

They wanted expression; they wanted life.
I let the brush find its way,
it became a scalpel, dangerous to those with self-doubt,
it struck my arms,
the blood not warm and forgiving,
but predatory
enjoying the flight of dreams, soaking deep into the
canvas.

The raven made an echoing croak,
and dashed away.
A tear rolled down my cheek,
it was not mine.

Dreams, Dreamers, and Dream Lovers

Dawn has not decided what mood the day shall have.
The sky is contemplative blue
but towering cumulus clouds are gathering.
Gentle waves almost touch the break wall.
Across the lake, autumn colors vary with the breezes.
You were always a vibrant red splashed on bright sunny yellows.
A portrait of passion and warmth.
I am layered in sad grays,
ill-defined, even beyond the canvas.

When we met, lilacs were about to bloom.
You hair changed from almond to butterscotch,
from shoulder length to face forming.
I never asked about your ring, you never asked about my scars.
We disagreed on what writers were the best, you said, "Emily Bronte."
You frowned when I said, "Poe."

You tossed your short white dress and white panties to
the bedroom chair.
You stretched one leg, then spread the other, cautioning,
"Remember hope is a cage."
My lips ignored the warning.

Summer began to ebb.
I was tethered to the thought of you.
To the need of you.
One morning the ducks from the lake took flight.
Not too many mornings afterward, you were gone.

My inclinations about dreams, dreamers, and dream
lovers
have all fragmented.
There is no mystery to loneliness,
it was Emily who created Heathcliff,
and Poe who said,
"Nevermore."

Chagall and Cezanne are just Names on Coffee Cups

I am never quite present when I need a word to qualify
its meaning.
I remain distant, squint-eyed,
vacillating between absent and apologetic.
You daydream, watching snowflakes,
wishing they were liberators.

The names Lady Day and Bird mean nothing to you,
and Chagall and Cezanne are just names on coffee cups.

When I ask for the meaning of contrition,
you shrug your shoulders, look away, and try to shake
the numbness.

You carelessly leaf through my copy of Macbeth,
resuscitating my failures, leaving no room for reveries.
Since I am incapable of intellectual restraint,

failed relationships resurrect themselves at the edges of
my mind.
They come forward to mingle with more self-destructive
thoughts,
and I fall prey to my vulnerabilities.
That is when life and imaginings become blurred,
and you slam the bedroom door behind you.

In a place full of memories and mirrors, our images
linger between a care and a tear.
I reflect on
a kiss,
a when,
a contradiction.

Once, you saw yourself in love with me,
now,
knowing me grates against every moment.

When I try to explain about contrasting parallels,
using examples from Wuthering Heights, you smile.

That sad, sweet smile that says commitment dies on the eve of triumph
when triumph never materializes.

The songs you listen to are foreign to me,
a jumble of words that cry out for false pity.
A pandering about money and a disdain for living.

When I ask for explanations, you declare with smugness,
"I never ran naked through a field of buttercups trying to catch butterflies
or
slid a razor across my wrists."

I Never Finished Loving You

On a beach,
under a crescent moon
while stars were dreaming
I kissed your lips.

Seasons changed,
and storms occurred.

When I shed all the personalities, I hid behind
you called me, "A stranger, unraveling in the dark."
When you asked me to leave, I felt the sadness you felt
for me,

Seasons change,
and storms occur.

When the clutter of the past
becomes a character in my mind
I simply choose to dance with recollections.

At other times
a splash of gold bursts on sunshine yellow
and I realize,
I never finished loving you.

The Venom in me

Not your fault,

the venom in me.

If I stay,

I will only

find new ways

to hurt you,

not because I don't love you,

I do,

But I hate myself more.

The wounds, long scars,

never healed,

the pain of being me

never subsided.

No matter how

the starlight captures your beauty,

the clenching bitterness

of

sorrow remains.

Slick Devil

I never found
daytime comfortable.
Replete with variations of greens,
distracting yellows
and bright oranges and reds.
I am content in the seams
where ashen prevails
against the grey
and dim figures are illusions
swallowed by the gloom.

At night,
in the weak starlight
I am preoccupied with
shadow and soul.
Deliberating poetry and suicide
with the slick devil
that resides in my mind.
He directs me toward paths of jagged shards,

and I coax him to follow.

I Lied When I told the Truth

I lied when I told the truth.
I never thought you would think about me afterward.

You lying naked on the couch.
My head resting between your legs.
One sad ballad after another playing in the background.
Even with open windows, the room was stuffy,
another breezeless summer evening.

When I brought you another vodka and soda,
you had already dressed.
I knew
that you knew I cared.
But you also knew,
I am a casualty of my own making.

Only flashes remain of how it began
when I promised we would race like cheetahs
and never hunger to uncover secrets.

You didn't open your mouth when you kissed me
goodbye.
You left quickly, and even the darkness
looked for an escape
not to surround me.

The Last Time I saw you

By Lorna Thomson & Philip Butera

The last time I saw you, we were in a dream.
We were shadowed in swirling hues of reds.
As our eyes met, you kissed me.
I was nude, and you had a kite in your hands.
I remembered how it feels to be alive.

Shrugging off, slumbered trivialities,
we stepped from all uncertainty
to meet in the grace of light.
You gave the kite to a little boy
who was walking his dog.
I wanted them to find their own dream,
there was only room for our desire in mine.

We become meteors screaming across the sky.
We become ocean waves rising and thrashing against the shore.
We were lovers,

tenderly and forever tethered.

I wanted to remain with you in that dream,

till dreams became stories told a million years from now.

I never wanted to miss you again.

Uncertain Translation

When the moon is hidden behind a sky of puffy gray clouds, I wonder whether it is waxing like we used to be or waning like we are doing now.

You walk ahead of me, wearing the distressed blue jeans with the cuts above the knees and across the calves.

You look younger, thinner, and not connected to me at all.

From the door, you drop your red bag with some designer initials on the blue leather chair atop your magazines that explain little.

You pour vodka over ice.

The dog is excited to see us, but you don't notice.

He, like me, is a nuisance these days. He sheds as collies do.

You complain about his long white hair on everything,

and when I ask questions about us,

the words are of uncertain translation.

How are the stones created? The silent, invisible ones we hurl

when we discover mirrors deceive, and life is fickle.
Yet, when all is waxing, nothing is seen.
We run toward horizons and ignore the distance.
Everything is soft, even judgment.
When waning, we become defenders of all we possess,
even ourselves.
I hesitate to ask about your doctor's visit because
everything becomes my fault.
The fading moonlight, the dog's hair, and my inability to
articulate
that I will love you forever,
with
or without your breasts.

The Language of my Mind

The cafe is quiet,
I remember being here,
the drinks,
kisses at the bar,
laughter,
my hand under your skirt,
promises being made.

Now, alone
the language of my mind
replays our romantic fantasy.
Driving to Montreal during springtime,
sailing to Victoria from San Francisco in summer.
In Fall, we were going to build a big bonfire at the beach,
and watch the sparks ask permission
of the heavens to enter.

When I attempt to reject my vanity
the roaring voice in my head

reminds me, it was I not you
that tore happiness from pleasure.
I want to slice my flesh,
watch the blood run
and listen to the echoes
of its cries.

Poets Shouldn't Drive Cars

Poets shouldn't drive cars.
They should pilot skyrockets.
Engines spewing words, and plumes of metaphors
creating stories about romance and wildness.

Poets are explorers above the clouds,
their curiosity leading them
beyond all that is wonderous into realms
where the mysteries of bliss
caress all that can be lyrical.

As the fiery sun has no language,
and dreams have no possessions,
poets are oracles, rendering destiny's moods.
Their words appear on streams of moonlight
fashioning time, with edginess
like Plato intended, and Homer excelled.

Poets capture the sky's imagination

writing poems that make the stars sparkle

and strangers fall in love with art.

In the Dream, Within a Dream

In the dream,
within a dream,
my mother appears.
I ask, "Am I in this dream?"
She says, "Why?"
Because the distance is abstract and I am
no longer asleep.

The dream within a dream
became the dream I was dreaming.
It was flawed
except for you, ethereal and wild.
I tried, but I could not catch you,
you were dreaming your own dreams.

I dreamt while dreaming
that from the periphery of the dream
the thing I feared most
would come true.

My mother

would disappear.

And you

become a dream.

I Wanted to Say, what she Already Knew

I wore thick wool socks,
and heavy boots laced firmly.
Flannel shirt, with herringbone vest,
and tweed ivy cap.
I began on the path
and quickly found myself bogged in mud.
I read the directions, *Continue, move backward to move forward.*
The air was thick and dank.
I was not on the road less traveled
but a well-journeyed trench.
Soon, I was soiled brown
and indistinguishable from those who forged before me.
We all must continue to learn,
it is said.

I wanted a short-cut.
To be immediately awakened

from my screams,
and part of the distance that never vanishes.
Once I grasped the truth
I noticed her.
She was half-naked, sunning herself
near a gentle waterfall.
She had gained weight,
over the years that had past.
Her breasts were heavier, her waist thicker.
Her face rounder but her large green eyes
remained clear and icy.
She was hope and hope is what I needed.
A moment to catch up, to see me through her eyes.
Usually, hope was on the move
heading to where I desired to be.

When she noticed me,
I laughed because she was smiling.
She said, “I knew you’d arrive,
after the others,
because you’re vain

and stubborn."

Memories can distance one from oneself.
Time is best packaged, wrapped, and left for others to interpret.

In her small summery cottage,
after sweet food and white wine,
we undressed.
Her movements hadn't changed.
I wondered if she ever thought of those days,
when it was easy to lose yourself in wishes.
When life was a journey toward something easy to imagine.

I drifted to sleep and dreamt of colors,
nourishing colors of hope.
I dreamed of capturing the sky,
transforming it into words,
giving poems to everyone I met
and watching them smile.

At dawn, when I attempted
to kiss below her waist
she brought my head up.
She wanted me to have something to desire.
Everything about her smelled of honey amber,
and she knew
that scent would linger with me,
that someday, when I was coming undone,
tumbling,
honey amber would be a reminder
of how honied and beautiful,
time with hope could be.
I wanted to say, what she already knew
but that's not what searchers do.

She gave me a clean white shirt,
and dark jeans with a field knife in the back pocket.
In a gilded mirror,
I saw myself as a habit I could never shed.

I held her close as we kissed at the door.
I didn't want to let her go, I thought if I only had the right words
I could tell her how frightened I was to travel without her.
The distance was ripe with shadows,
but when the sun is bright, shadows are expected.
She said, "Once you leave there are no paths,
no roads,
no directions,
no excuses,
and I won't be here if you return.
But, I might, might be found
at the destination
you are seeking."

If Stars are Diamonds

If stars are diamonds, why can't I have one?
If clouds are filled with kisses, where are mine?
At night, I hear the wind whisper my name.

Reflections wrap themselves in innocence
and moments cling to distances.
In my dreams, I search the sky
hoping to find meaning.
Thunder roars and lightning leads the way.
I catch sight of who I should have been
but when I run to replace myself
I awake.

Dawn breaks into colors,
time and imagination stir.
The mirror shows me
standing next to myself
with you at the edge
running toward the moon.

Her Cold Eyes Full of Hatred

The notion of eternity:
twilight without darkness,
no dangers, no fragmentation,
no more winters,
no more lovers disappearing.

Angelic caresses flit through my mind.
Our anticipation of being together
becoming a path, we treasured.
Two dreamers searching for meaning.

Yet, under you lie her,
a thread beginning, a tragedy of the imagination,
fumbling unadorned contradictions, trembling over rainbows,
dissolving, embracing allusions illuminating.

Now, exiled, my wounds lengthen,
I laugh at the laughter in my mind,

whether metaphors or metaphysics.
She was a beautiful conquest,
wrapped in deceitful lust.
We three, steeped in a charade,
having one, then the other.
The taste of bliss lingering on our lips.

Then heartbreak,
was it your legs or hers
spread wide
prepared for creation?

Even today,
I cannot see what is behind me.
The storm continues, the innocent improvising.
Beyond our passion, past any doubt, I still hear your voice
screaming for her.
Loving what you could never understand,
that stars are misplaced when dreaming.

As recollections call,

not in a reverie

but adorned in ceaseless repetition

I see myself undressing you.

My tongue a rogue scorpion in crevasses corrupt and wretched.

Sweet from night-scented flowers,

we found endless ways never to be innocent.

Ghosts escape innuendos

though they reside in beds.

We were a contradiction,

your mistress, you and me,

daring characters who knew

brief love and danger before.

Time twists our images.

Your lips on mine,

her arm around your waist.

A young woman opening a door,

dagger in hand
her cold eyes full of hatred.
Without saying a word,
we chose damnation
over redemption
as the mirror shattered.

I am Stitched Together

I am not
the mirror's image
confident and smiling,
I am behind
the silvery illusion
locked in contradiction,
a gliding contour and
a plague of indifference.
I am stitched together
by my words,
words familiar and words discouraging.

I am neither whole
nor mad
but a curious intruder
vexed by my reflection.

I Imagine Myself as a Solitary Albatross

Death suits me,
the long relentless solitude.
No scowls of discouragement,
only languid obscenities from a mind broken from illusions.
I am comfortable between voids
where a violin with barbed-wire strings accompanies reminiscences.

There is no pain, merely the scars.
My mind shifts between what has been abandoned and what never was.
Safe from hope, without dreams, sleep is restful.
Though at times, the warmth of being, flutters,
and I imagine myself as a solitary albatross, a distance from nesting…
whose muddy feet keep him from soaring.
The circumstances change, but not the tragedy,
I am still me.

I have Allowed Myself to Shine

I am bursting,

but the mirror shows no reflection.

I am under the influence of dreams.

At the table,

chairs are pulled back for breakfast

and pushed forward after dinner.

I shout to those near,

they hear nothing.

They don't see me expanding,

elongating and

becoming.

I have allowed myself to shine.

Turn off the television,

toss away those earphones.

See my brush touch the canvas.

See me ignite.

I am freeing all the colors I have suppressed.

The tangled reds, mysterious purples, bursting oranges,

the grays that have a tear attached

and the loneliest color of all, white.

White, with infinite versions of itself.

No, I will not labor.

My job is to think.

To create

what hauntingly

never ceases to astound.

I am an artist

using graceful lines of poetry to court the mannered

dressed in elegance.

I am at the center

sipping champagne in stemware

while

wide-eyed admirers

pursue me.

In my world, it is never time for sleep,

It is star time

for I am

bursting.

Always a Stranger

My past is wrapped in tumbles and escapes.
I see me but in shadow,
arranging seasons,
the distance always unclear yet
in motion.

Short black skirt, blue eyes, breasts moist from my lips.
I loved you.
As styles changed, we grew apart.
You wedded, had children, planted a garden.
I remained on the train,
clinging to nightfall, arrogant and brooding,
charmed by expectations.

Under thin cotton sheets,
you on me, then me on you,
we were the moment, challenging assumptions
and reinventing adjectives

to exaggerate our self-importance.
I was always a stranger to myself
while you
completed your reflection.

The train clatters across a trestle,
in the club car, finishing a drink
I hear myself demanding more of me.
I dissect metaphors from allegories anticipating your
entrance.
I fall from the cross into your arms,
but it is not you.
She has red hair and bright eyes.
Just another among others,
listening to me as if I were Dorian Gray.

Mysteries are contradictions
and a thousand questions remain unanswered.
In mirrors, on shattered glass, and in the stars,
you appear, a smile from the past.
While every image of me parallels moments in time,

all these images merge into who I should have been.

You gently kiss my lips.

I linger, knowing what I feel, is not what I want.

And I,

move on.

A Wolf in a Fox Hole

I could never depend on myself,
I didn't particularly like me.
I find being me confining,
like a wolf in a fox hole.

When comfort is needed
I never look to myself for help.
Morning's sunlight greets me,
but I like the night.
Dark places where I could shed me,
walk into a bar
and feel welcomed.

Once, after many drinks
I caught a glimpse of me
talking with a slender woman
with cold dark eyes.
I was outraged.
I waited until I saw me heading for the restroom.

I followed.
I did not recognize me.
I never hated anyone more than I hated myself.
As I primped in the mirror, I struck.
My stiletto blade went across the throat,
I was mesmerized watching me stagger, the blood streaming out.
I reached for me to help,
I pushed myself to the floor, I was elated.
I wanted a souvenir, so I took my mind.

The bar had become a courtroom.
The judge was black, and the jury was white
I called my first witness, Poe, he said, "Read me."
Next, I called Freud, who said, "Reality is a cause, dreaming the effect."
Traceable impressions became confessions.
I was acquitted.

My disappearance caused no outcry.
The lonely remained lonely.

The slender woman was a doctor,
she said, “sex is indifference
bored with itself.”
I asked if we had ever met before,
she said, “lovers are strangers
soon to be friends.”
But at the fringes, I could feel me
re-emerging.
I bought a gun.

Images Interrupt Dreams

I am mad
from thinking.
I am disenchanted with illusions.
I pace my mind
but
disconcerting images interrupt dreams.

Clouds become ellipses,
thoughts harangue.
I cling to me,
a cataclysm in a spiraling descent
distracted
only
by nightmares.

I sat there Thinking, always Thinking

Who am I?
I asked myself.
I recall meeting myself one morning for breakfast.
I sat there thinking, always thinking.
I asked myself if I minded the intrusion.
I had no feeling about this encounter.
I was gloomy and pretentious to myself.
I ignored me until my feelings burst through my
thoughts.
"Why are you there and not here?" I asked.
"I could ask that also," I answered.
We both thought past what was once illogical,
wondering if we were each other or both the
same.

San Francisco Sailed to France

Could you imagine the insanity
if words and colors
were not freed by Ferlinghetti
and San Francisco
sailed to France?
Gauguin would have fought in the Tenderloin,
while Van Gogh napped
under the Golden Gate.

Peach Colored Cheeks

On a summer's evening
behind a roller coaster
the girl from the lost and found
with peach-colored cheeks
wearing a short denim skirt and a threadbare blouse too
tight
brought me to a lonely beach cottage that smelled of
rotting wood and mildew.
I watched her undress, there were no words,
I had not learned the language yet.
Her lips were thin and dry,
but soft as they lingered on my face.
Young and impressionable
I had no idea I was held together
by the weight
of ten thousand tears

Our lives
are a plight of incoherence,

where time is never a friend.
The rain erases the words and gusts turn the pages.
We move,
leaving behind what should be treasured
for what is misunderstood.
We step,
through tragedies of our own making
becoming possessed by our blindness.
We seem to never
just be,
just be.

The sun in January struggles,
it never appears very bright.
The gray clouds take control,
snowflakes greet each other at my window.
I sit in a dark leather chair,
a thick flannel shirt over a turtleneck.
There are no words to accurately describe
fallen angels from our past.
The mysteries of splendor and misfortune,

have become the heavy boots of knowing,

and god,

god

is just another

grain of sand disappearing

in an hourglass.

Next to Panties, Next to Flesh

I am plagiarized, I can not find myself,
I see a rose, real in mind, plastic in reality.
Flames consume my vision, though the fire is only a
rumor.
I can't listen anymore, I hate pretense.
I keep my head between female legs
next to panties, next to flesh,
real things.
I am told, all are consumed with possibilities,
some parade,
some leave the pavement for pavilions.
Preceding decades were performances of prodigious art,
invention, and wars.
The present is thoughtless, a nightmare pulled from a
bad dream.
I am not an argument but an announcement,
there are programs, positions, and places,
then again
I have tried

and

I have found

there is a plague

upon every path.

I Gamble with Priests

Across the harbor, at a tavern, red and blue neon lights are visible.
I gamble with priests there, they take my money and bless my soul.
The priests say I am vulnerable because there are no prayers for what I want.

My black dog and I study art together, I read Poe, he examines statues.
We travel up and down the line, sometimes we cross it.
When priests tell me luck is God's gift, I ask about the martyrs.

Sometimes as I drink beer and write poetry, my dog courts a gray and white collie.
The collie is owned by a tall lady with short yellow hair who sings at the church.
While our dogs amuse each other, we watch seagulls play above the waves.

Her cottage and breath smell like cinnamon tea, her
breasts, and legs smell like sesame oil.
She told me she once painted cabins, in harvest fields
against snow-capped mountains.
She seemed to always be available when God was
nowhere to be found.

The lady took our dogs to live with her in a small beach
town in Ontario.
I miss laying in her small bed under the white sheets,
which were dried by the sea breezes.
The bar where I drink beer is still visited by priests who
ask more of me than I can give.
When I get home, a ginger and white cat cannot be seen.
Dogs greet you,
but cats are skeptical.
I call the cat, "Chance" since her eyes reveal she is
determining whether or not to give me away.

Once I Jumped

A poet friend,
who never reads her work,
told me her pain was white.
White,
the color of sheets, towels,
and dress shirts of my youth.
I can picture my mother, in a white blouse
tossing white clothes from piles on the cold basement floor
into the double concrete laundry sink filled with water and bleach.
The intense smell blending with the mildewed odors from the dank walls.
My mother, her face glistening with a thin layer of sweat
swishing the combination with a well-worn wooden pole.
White is something that has to be kept up,
white is distinct,
essential things are white

birth and death certificates.
Souls and canvases start out white.

White is the color of foolishness,
a welcomed dancer in a sky of blue,
and white is always a friend.
Friend and welcomed
are warm words,
they are smiles at daybreak.
But I know the voice in my head is not white,
it is deep indigo.
Indigo, meaning truthfulness.
When I open my flesh and see the futility
of white, tangled among reds, purples, and pinks,
so anxious to escape
tears come to my eyes.
My vision turns to watery silver,
and all that I see
is not what I imagine white is like.

Often, on gray days,

when I am trying to understand God,
I stand below a trestle and wait for me to jump.
I wave to the solitary figure of myself,
trying to capture my attention,
to let myself know,
when varied greens and
contemplative yellows
splash through my thoughts
then,
I know with certainty
I am not broken,
but
that is not often.

Once I jumped from the trestle
I was saved by a woman,
all in white.
She caught me in her arms,
with a loving kiss.
When I asked, "when will I see you again?"
she said, "are you seeing me now?"

I think,
what if death is bleaker than madness?

A cold wind blows rain all around me.
I see through a haze, the white flesh of things without
feeling connected.
I cannot understand
why my friend believes
white is the color of pain.
It is the color of distance, of anticipation,
it is without blemishes.

Black, is my color
the color of bonds and chains of a heart that feels,
not at all
or never enough.
Black is the color of absence,
when I imitate myself in the company
of those who wear white, I am never discovered,
because like all strangers to themselves
I am not there.

I am on that trestle

just as a snow-white shrouded train

races past.

A Lemon Sepia Remembrance

On the patio of a café
I overheard an attractive woman
say, “Somewhere yesterday.”

The clanging began, incessant clanging,
like tributaries from a million shadows.
The rain had stopped,
but the smell of rain remained.
Is it Vancouver, I recall?
I stare into my past,
the collusions and collisions of my journeys.
In a crowded nightclub
under blue-green lights I catch glimpses,
wondering if I met myself,
would I recognize
me?

The moist wind wafts a sweet flowery fragrance,
reminding me of a psychologist's bare breasts,

warm and pink
resting on Cohen's Spice Box.
She giggled when she spread her legs.
Looking back, they all seemed to giggle.
They were real,
made of flesh and tears.
I have always been an outsider,
aloof, even from myself,
a sharp shard of stained-glass,
with slight nuances of reds and blood orange.

In Lake Tahoe,
the snow fell
until the night was dawn.
White clouds, white world,
whiteness surrounded me.
On a small round mirror
with
white lines and white pills
I removed my appearance.
A friend watched,

she sighed
before
gathering her clothes and moving on.

There are no vertical or horizontal,
only reams of remembrances uncurling,
coloring the past,
yet they remain.

I have scars from those hawks and doves
that made their way through me.
My lovers once adventurous,
now businessmen's wives,
slightly over-weight
turning pages in their children's private lives,
maybe recalling me.

In a small room, in an old hotel
in Buffalo,
a cautious woman with large blue eyes
spoke and drank for hours before she allowed

my lips to venture below her belly.
She tasted like my youth, sweet and never-ending.
I was coming back from where I had been
not absolved yet less guilty.
When I awoke, she was gone
When I called, she said
she enjoyed being led astray,
but her wildness was fleeting.

Age dispels illusions.
I am between phases,
between sublime madness and reflection,
but still on the run, a sutured dreamer,
a lemon sepia remembrance
searching for a final soliloquy.

The waiter places my drink
on a summery themed coaster.
The attractive woman gathers her things.
My mind repeats,
"Somewhere yesterday,"

I smile,

as the rain begins again.

We Made Pumpkin Pie in July

I have grown tired of cinnamon.
I prefer butterscotch, thick, unambiguous, full of promises.
You left four bars of sandalwood soap behind.
I followed the scent when I needed to find you.
There always seemed to be hints of autumn in our house.
We made pumpkin pies in July.

I gave away
the unfinished drawings you left behind,
just like you gave me away.
Tossed to the wind, to the night, to the melancholy of late fall.
You said you were tired of dreaming, and you wanted to feel.

Strangling vines, once green are now brown,
the whole garden will be crumbling soon.
I miss being beside you,

listening to you talk about the colors of Western Canada.
How your Canadian accent would come alive and on
those moments,
I longed to crawl inside you, bathe in the love you felt
for things imagined.
I wanted to brand your smile on my heart,
but we never took that trip to Vancouver.
Soon the snow will come, I will sit by the lake
watch as it freezes, occasionally spotting a fox
and crafting images of us
that never took place.

A Bitter Taste in my Heart

I am never around

when

I need me.

I am distant

when

I need comfort.

I have traveled away from me,

looking for myself without clues of returning.

I once heard me say, "I have waited too long,"

I was young then, without boundaries

but

I misstepped, I drifted into my illusions,

self-contained,

in a poem, in a dream,

wrapped in a fantasy.

I caught a glimpse of her,

her perfect face, her sexy walk.

My pursuit began,
away from whom I might become.
I separated the future from the past,
replenishing the now.
Passion never needs permission,
it lingers long after logic retreats.
Time became just moments fleeting,
one quicker than the last.

Since love is like delicate lace,
only fragments remain.
A word, a thought, a happenstance
and
a bitter taste in my heart.

I Never Hide, but I am Hidden

The train leaves the station,
yet I know,
there is no one aboard
I have kidnapped them for a story I need to write.

The passengers start a bonfire
by a lake.
The night has a haze, made hazier by the smoke.
A tall, blue-eyed woman from the Club Car joins us.
I offer her wine, but she wants Grand Marnier.
She follows me into the cabin,
One hand holds a revolver,
the other unbuttons her blouse,
when I approach,
she says, "I never hide, but I am hidden."

I tap the pencil to my chin,
searching for the next line.

Chariots too Fast to Catch

Lights,

like wide mouth jars are scattered above the stage.

Tiny fragments float in the air twinkling both dull gray

and polished silver.

Ladies in folding chairs flare their nostrils.

I peer from the edge of a gauzy curtain.

I am between pillars, fearing Samson's fate.

Someone has called "The Poet."

Out there,

menacing birds will observe their prey.

I am a palette of awakening colors.

Glass, in one hand, scars on the other.

My ambitions erupted from dreams and have become

chariots too fast to catch.

I am alone, a thin silk thread.

My words joust, sometimes sweet and at other times,

bitter.

They are calling, "The Poet."

Destiny,

like a tin can pried open with a knife, leaves sharp edges

that cut deep into the flesh.

I kick at sadness, and I distrust happiness.

I discard both and scowl at my distorted reflection in

sepia mirrors.

You see, time is a sin pocketed by sleepwalkers.

Where brilliant poets like I

contemplate murdering

those who miscomprehend nakedness.

The appropriate words will always be mine to give.

I am,

The Poet.

When I can go no Further

The weight of madness descends further,
I have become someone else.
This dispair is familiar
I see myself in the corner,
a whiteness surrounds me.
I take my hand and descend
below the levels where the mad have gone insane
and the insane consider their madness.
When I can go no further,
at the end of all things,
God's Creator is among all the dead.
She is large and naked, sitting atop layers of corpses.
Moans from the hopeless are heard, yet a cold emptiness
surrounds her.
As I pick up the fragments of who I was
I begin to understand,
life is crafted isolation.
When I ask, "Am I beyond what is?"
I am shown all my tears, and all the tears I am yet to cry.

RACING TO A MIRROR

I HAVE IMAGININGS TUCKED IN ENVELOPES
I HAVE NEEDS ARRANGED IN STARS
I WILL BE WHO I THINK I AM.

THERE ARE RIPPLES BEFORE THE CLARITY,
AND SENTIMENT OVER REFLECTIONS.
IT IS JUST A MATTER OF TIME
BEFORE THE SUN RISES.
I WILL DANCE FROM MY DREAMS
ARTICULATING MY AMBITIONS.

I WILL BE ON PARADE,
CRESTING ON A WAVE
OUT FROM DARKNESS
RACING TO A MIRROR
TO SEE
IF I HAVE BECOME
WHO I AM.

Caught in a Ceaseless Gale

With my finger,
I trace blue ink lines on a pink pad.
You are gone,
you are sorry.

Waves crash,
this is a hurricane
the green fields, and young saplings
scream to be unearthed and moved,
to be saved,
but they remain.
The raging floodwaters engulf
what is alive and what was once imagined.

In a distant landscape,
caught in a ceaseless gale,
red threads trail a fragile tapestry.
Is that you escaping
or me unraveling?

Words

The men in expensive suits with influence carefully crafted
what had transpired
with words so eloquent, they must be true.
What was left, those words which growl, expose and contradict
were rushed away.
They were wrapped in gauze and placed in a stained glass box.
The box
was placed in a red circle.
The circle was eased into a more significant blue square.
All other polygons were discarded.
Finally, a white star was found, and the square was hidden beneath its center.

Horns heralded the wordsmiths
for their oratory.
A triumph was declared

because the words were so convincing.

As I approached an old wooden clock
that no longer showed the time.
I noticed a word peeking from behind it.
It was not a kind word.
In fact, a small cadre of somber words was hiding.
They had escaped
before the box was put away.
Mostly nouns and verbs, but other parts of speech
were present.
They were all frightened
because if they were discovered
justifications would be needed,
and during that discourse
what had been discarded would become compromised.
There would be questions, both overruled and sustained.
Witnesses with serious faces would be called and asked
to swear to what they knew had transpired.
Someone with a deep voice in authority would say these
are directionless words and

make a statement charging that what is wrong can never
be correct
if what is right is not.
Nouns would be disbelieved first,
then the verbs changed from present to past tense,
making their claim before the incident
disputed.
It would be shown these words were compromised.
The crowd would disband, happy with the original
words
that were used.
The words that had escaped were all erased.

Later, while I was
pondering why the words that were used on such
occasions always sounded the same,
without complication
and
without a doubt,
I noticed a star flickering
as if crying.

I gently held it.
From inside, I heard voices.
I carefully unpacked
what was needed
and opened the box.
Tears now filled my eyes.
All the words were shivering and feverish.
Some had already succumbed.
One word, badly misused
asked if I knew who they were.
I didn't.

The word, and the rest of the words
took refuge inside me,
they filled my mind
and mingled with my thoughts
before long
the word that was abused
came forward.
He looked through my eyes at the world
I saw.

The word told me lies were always pretty,

they are gifts from those with power.

Un-lies

break loud and alarm,

for revealing the truth

requires a benefit.

A Knot Tied Tight, Moored to Nothing Secure

"The dog still drinks with his ears in the water bowl." What more can I say?

I thought I was stronger, but I was shattered when hours passed, days, then months, and you never returned.

You were always refining your predatory skills. I was but a moment, a blurred image when you needed to feel rewarded. I was just me, a knot tied tight, moored to nothing secure.

One afternoon, I saw blood under the dog's eye. He wasn't frightened, I was. The dice roll, and I am always apprehensive when they stop and reveal the many that lose and the few that win.

The Veterinarian told me the dog's cut would heal. Let it dry, a scab forms, and then a small scar will remain. I feel like I have been a scar since birth, a character I invented to play me. I act, and when night arrives, I put fabric over all the mirrors, and heavy drapes conceal the windows. When I am sure the darkness and I are one, I disembark from me. I leave the body you see and the face I hate. I become the sound of a cello tuned in perfect fifths: from low to high. I am not loud but haunting, projecting a tone that states I am comfortable here. My harmonic is carefree and escapist. I enjoy not being me. I am grateful, cheerful, and I am not an overtone directed to compliment anyone's folly.

My pleasing sound captures the mood of the house, its warmth, and its appeal. Though at times, I become frightened because I can feel you nearby, bold and unforgiving, more expressive than I could ever accomplish. Your scowl and appetite turn capriciousness into hard discordance. When this happens, I hear my echo, the weight of disenchantment far exceeding the tenderness of believing.

Winter turned into a wet spring. This summer has been cooler than most. Your hair has more blonde highlights, and your lovely face still captures attention. You come close to looking happy, but we know that can only happen at another's expense.

Friends tell me you have traveled to my favorite city, Vancouver. Naturally, you saw its beauty and became jealous. You wanted to conceal the snow-capped Coastal Mountains and make the clouds over Stanley Park darker than your hatred for all things you view as a challenge to your beauty. I hope when I visit again, you haven't stained the city, making it less authentic.

A Dental Specialist pulled out two of the dogs decaying front teeth, so the tip of his tongue always seems to be showing a bit of pink in a pleasing white face. His big dark eyes are still bright, and when we are alone at night, he does not always run to the front window when he hears a car anymore. He mostly just looks at me, waiting for us to take a long walk and understand how lucky we are to have each other.

Before and After the War

Sometime during the night while I was sleeping, my head exploded. When I awoke, I saw me, alone, dreams shattered. I reached for my hand, but I rejected myself. Outside thunder and lightning were chattering nonsense, their bravado wrapped in cathartic accolades.

Is that me walking between the exploding bombs, unraveling before the alarm sounds? I see where I am still sleeping, wide awake in dreams about nightmares. Over the radio, theatrical companies announce the death of sanity. They say it was a waste of time, even God walked off the set. I shake me once more, my body asks why?

"Didn't you know?" Is the echo from an answer I had given myself many years ago. Before I fully realize the pain inside me, my refection slips away from the mirror. Sad and sorry about my absence, I continue to sleep. Tears fill my eyes, roll down my face into the consequences I am to experience when I awake or when I fall asleep.

I am gone, and my lover is alone, we are just a discourse my friends are having among themselves. I contemplate the history of the scalpel, there is always something sharp to be appreciated. Things sharp make statements, create emotions, confirm punishment, and gives reason to wonder, while blood becomes art. And art is the space between genius and insanity, an eclipsing river that is pregnant for tributaries, but creativity is needed, and thoughts become too precious to share.

There is no revelation, only agony, and when you see yourself through my eyes, the night becomes paralyzed, and illusions are confiscated. I look at me, drunk with ineptitude, filling no niche close to worthwhile, I sneer at the injustice of being me, though being anyone else would still carry the sting of insignificance.

On stage, I am the softness of brilliant light, leaving one dream to enter another. You can see me, frightened as

I appear from mere rhetoric. I observe the sentiment, I absorb what rational thinking deems unfit, then I am abandoned along with the reason.

As dogs bark and cats signal angels to fly from this dream into holographic visions, backgrounds are wiped clean of erasing where every warm dawn shadows death, and interrogations are given of the dying who have never lived.

Before being crucified, I am questioned, I say, “My love crafts images,” you respond snickering, “ You could not get my nakedness out of your mind.” Which is true. Either way, naked or waiting on the powerful but illiterate, nails are pounded into every sentence I make, and when I protest that I could speak for myself, a spike finds my heart. It is not very bloody, more like a short story no one will ever read.

Introspecting on a reverie, I insist you wrap your naked legs around my face, the smell gives you away, just as I did. We are on the outskirts stampeding with buffalos, Wagner can be heard on loudspeakers. Being with you unimagines all my thoughts. You are enthusiastic. Telling the philistines war is a game of penalties when suddenly a fragment of barded wire embeds itself in my eye. My mouth opens, and toreadors exit giving me the sight to hear all my mistakes crying to make me whole again.

In pain, I think, I think about thinking, I ride the Ferris wheel with vengeful gods, who tell me about the boys they bed, and I tell them about the merciless gods I skewer and feed to honeymoon couples who wake too late to understand their sanity is being drained from them. The wind whirls, suppressing evidence, revealing deficiencies. Repelled, I retreat into the disillusionment of being alive, with my mind opened, I recognize the sea and Jesus walking on it. My queries ride the waves to him, but his replies smash into break walls disappearing between the acts of knowing and the impossibilities of understanding.

Traveling quicker than false definitions, I shed my old skin, casting off the sins my mother said I never made, but my father just laughed. He knew his son was an unbearable anchor tied to him. I was not the cleanliness of hope, but a forever waste of my mother's milk that should have been given to a radiant sister who always created smiles. In a jungle where words never connect and time is a blind gladiator, there is a progression of written waste. I look for the sun at night to save the spurned, but I am trapped. I, as me, inside coils, inside roseries faltering to recognize my presence, just like my father.

My body surfaces in a barroom with a thousand stab wounds, yet one more is needed. I am told as I am being stripped and whipped, love is just an equation of judgment. Standing in the distance, in her dream, not mine, a beautiful woman with blonde hair and large bare breasts, hiding a scar on her ego, deals me into the game. She makes me swallow my interests in sex and has me playing against all the me's I have told myself I am.

While I speak of the mental anguish in *Crime and Punishment*, all my cards turn blank, and with a fist full of naked queens, the beautiful woman wins every hand. She says spending time between her legs is neither pleasure nor punishment, that at the furthest uncurling end of thoughts is something worth living or dying for. It was designed for adventurers who think the mind is too dangerous to think about. It is thought conforming to its own existence.

When what you see can't be explained and what you feel can't be expressed, the inquisition begins. Deep in a pit during REM sleep, at the center of my being, Saint Paul looks back after matching wits with Caligula. Both men raped the words before they used them and left them for dead. Frightened that the sky would blacken and fall, I returned to my birth to see if I had awakened. What remained was a shattered mirror reflecting me as a teenager reading, *"The Bell Jar."*

In my back pocket, there is a map of Baltimore where I plot to help Poe unbury his three mothers and search for Virginia in the city beneath the sea. When the haters of poetry arrive, I state, "I am a prism, fractured, lost in segregated dreams." Nevertheless, I am called a traitor, and I am named as a witness against all that prevailing tastes want to destroy, all art dreamed about, and all art that slays sanity. I simply state it was never an apple but a strawberry that Eve gave to me, aware of my enlightenment, hooves pound the earth and a tempest rages from the observer I had become, but juries are deceiving as Adam can attest too.

After the accusations that artwork had become the chaos of human dignity, the verdict became law. War was debated by those who never speak the truth, not even when their portraits are destroyed and their self-images detained. Eve and me, I in my mind, and Eve, even with a touch of madness, knew rejection was neither a consequence nor an exertion but a risk to stultify language. We rejected the confusion, and with her buttocks numb from kisses, she shook me, “Awake.”

I sit up on the bed, Eve takes her finger from her vagina and puts it in my mouth, I immediately dissect myself into feelings, images, and sensations. All pathological conditions, but I recognize I bathe in the celestial colors of ultramarine and vermillion, both are superior in capturing false thoughts and curing mental malfunctioning.

Perfect, I invite authors into my sanity; on skates, they cut deeply into my brain, till what I have known becomes what I will eventually conspire to master. I set out to widen my duality, I watch myself and me, lear at each other, one thinking the other will not understand what I am shouting in my sleep without Eve’s confirmation that I am my own dream.

“There was a window,” Eve, now the Birth of Venus states. “An interpretation in stained glass,” I draw concentric circles around celebrated passages of, *The*

Stranger. The sheer weight of incidental words are dangerous, they are melancholic scorpions and delusional black widows angrily attacking self-retribution. Endlessly destroying, endlessly maddening, the repetition continues, illiterate men chronicling their obsession with persecution, telling tales of stillbirths on the dawn of man's conception.

There is a disdain for reasoning, what is wanted is closed paths to expectation, I rustle, feeling somewhat unearthed and fortunate for the ideas I am experiencing. Then through the tunnels, the abyss, the stretch of momentous time I see you, you are Eve. All of your smiles now dispel all misconceptions. Your mask crumbles, and you escape. I see you, I see me, in the distance like it was, I see lanterns in the misty forest between the trees, I see you, I see me, I see us reveling in what can never be destroyed.

I awake, sweating, feeling traveled, and tired. Sometime during the night, during the war, while I was sleeping, my head exploded.

The Lonesome, feel the Contours of Darkness

The lonesome, feel the contours of darkness. They follow the aimless corridors of nighttime, never understanding their direction. Seeing halos and passing neon names on gravestones, with the same thoughts circling their minds. They bump into themselves with disinterest. Not wanting anyone near, having conversations about how a warm wind trails the hurricane, and ocean water is less cold than eyes that never catch your glazed glance.

It is night in Hawaii. Drapes are pulled tight, someone's god hangs from one small nail on the bathroom wall, telling me this is where living ends, and misery begins. I hear voices from other rooms talking about what might lie beyond the words of prophets who speak about being one with all possibilities. From promises to comparisons, Prometheus never understood the lyrics to any Dylan song, he just hummed one Cole Porter line about getting no kick from cocaine. When my mind was given back to me, from King Kamehameha,

I felt like an Indian Mongoose resting in rotting pineapples at Hanauma Bay.

The implications are clear. I have plagiarized myself withdrawing what I can't seem to hold dear to my heart. The original saying of, I need you is like a furious torrent of lava from Mauna Loa unaware its destination is itself. Like me running into misfit mariners at Pearl Harbour. They carry those glass wings that emerge from definitions of self and selflessness.

I beg you, use the gun, squeeze the trigger. Concerns about apostolic logic cannot prevent you from appreciating the outcome of brain matter converging to conceive the child we spoke about when you walked me to the gallows. We had just returned from the back street brothels in Waikiki. Where the sex experts needed help because aesthetic notions can take the place of sustenance when money is used to barter for expectations.

You had me strip down to my elemental thoughts, then the whip you used to contemplate discretion slapped across my back. The ecstasy of pain drove me to believe in foul characters in adventure novels. All my blood funneled to a chalice used to make discoveries about what nature has rejected. Then your other lover, the one with blonde hair and thick greedy lips, called my name. It was my turn to be chained at the pillar. Your smile rested atop my agony as the tacks dug into my flesh, exposing my emotions. I screamed I love you before my self-torturing romanticism gushed to liquid hatred. I had created myself a proper noun now, but verbs were needed for me to become an attendant of God. The God you said made you orgasm just by holding your attention. In the end, the native young and disfigured anti-heroes confiscated my errant ideas. Whores from other small islands shifted me away from myself. I had become who I believed could not take my place.

Under blankets, martyrs told me to slip away from my intellect and float past the first signals but to introduce myself to myself when the horses are in the stretch. That is the only time dice rolled honestly, and bullets are aimed straight at the riders. I came to see if there was a movement of the soul when Poe's eulogy is repeated. But I was alone and only offered likelihoods that Van Gogh may have never painted anything while he was sane.

On Sandy Beach, you were naked playing with the oracles of Delphi, I was locked in an instant that burns without fire. Your mouth was open, and your legs were spread. Surfers from Maui sang Gabby songs to contain their laughter. Moby Dick swallowed Pele. Then the sun defied logic, and I shivered, all the rules about wanting to be one with unpredictable spirits became vapors magicians use to distill moments from seconds.

Behind Heartbreak Sanatarium, I caught a catamaran to Suicide Manor on Desperation Isle. The Samoans have had lobotomies and can't feel the nooses around their necks, they just punish the quarry. No guests, no jukebox, no phones, and no witnesses. Each room has fire ants and scorpions to keep away the rats. I was tattooed by a woman without eyes who told me never to watch the waves; they are made of misconceptions. Copies of *"The Kingdom of Evil"* were everywhere, even in the galley where rum and bread are sold. Mango covered fishing hooks called communion are placed on slack guitar sheet music and forced down our throats. My nurse, who was naked from the waist down, was obsessed with Frankenstein's monster. She had knitting needles through her neck, and she repeated lines from Mallarme's poem:

> "And I feel that I am dying, and, through the medium
> Of art or of mystical experience, I want to be reborn,
> Wearing my dream like a diadem, in some better land
> Where beauty flourishes."

When I told her I understood, and I would take her to Kilauea, she basted herself in misconception and dived into a vat of water that changed to wine. She was served that evening after prayers. I requested what I liked before, her vagina. But I was told that treat was saved for the sailors who walked on water.

When I was made to confess, I asked about you, this articulate man with oriental eyes told me everyone has had you, they showed me movies of you dancing with Bacchus and a mighty ram trailing behind you. The man held himself with both hands and asked if I wanted to taste you by kissing his genitals? I screamed, "Stop, imitating me?" There was laughter, thunderous laughter, and a deep voice said, "Do you really think anyone is here?"

Coming towards me from Hana, I saw Blessed Mary's cousin Elizabeth. She offered me her small breasts, but the sustenance was gone. I asked about her sexual preferences, she handed me her tongue, unzipped my torso, and entered. I felt her removing the barbs you carefully placed when you said, "I needed you."

When I told my analyst, "I feel more not like me than like me," he had his young assistant fold his toilet paper, wipe him then flush the toilet. After tossing a wet paper towel into the waste bin, he looked at my reflection in the mirror and said, "Obviously, you have an idealized vision of yourself." His assistant told me to lay on the wet floor, she handed me her panties and dragged adverbs across my chest. They left holes for conventions of the past to be released. I could not cry; I could only cast doubt on my existence. I was hypnotized watching the removal of my psyche. It was placed in a coconut cave where abstract poets fight off protestant explorers.

Underneath the new Colossus, connecting Lahaina and Kaanapali, you met that couple from Eden. I was at sea with Kurtz searching for the end of the heart of darkness. You confessed the husband, Adam was dim-witted. When he undressed you, he made no attempt to praise your beautiful breasts. He just brought you fragrant flowers and asked about life outside the garden. While listening to a Tahitian choir, Adam delicately placed small vegetables between your buttocks then buried his tongue so deep inside you, a snake rushed from your mouth. His willowy Nordic wife, Eve, on the other hand, wanted to experience all of the excesses beyond dangerous. She refused to be a saint because the crudeness of their thinking was disconcerting, she alluded to the price of disenchantment - her one son killed the other. Without regret, all her lips were soft entrances into evolving deprivation, they swallowed away any plight replacing theology with the emergence of art itself.

I was at the back of the Luau. Against the wall drinking Absinthe, a dash of Pervitin, along with female ejaculate in a chipped Waterford champagne glass when Eve, Lady Macbeth, and you sauntered into the night club. I immediately knew you were about to commit crimes, so I put tiny bubbles in my ears. With collective charms, you were dangerous sirens, temptresses looking for prey. Lady Macbeth's long naked legs, Eve's greenish-gold eyes, and you, my love with an inviting mouth that could suck a heart from its chest. You three lured all the men to your table. Eve encouraged them to masturbate as all of you began to sing the sweetest, most enchanting sounds ever heard but never to be reheard. The men died as they lived, one indistinguishable from another.

I slipped into the Ladies room where women were enjoying each other in positions Fellini would have loved to film, if it were really happening. I was out the window, rushing through the alleys and into the arms of a haole nurse who sucked the liquid from my ears. She played the ukulele beautifully. She told a story about how the world is divided into clowns, butchers, and artists. I would have to make a choice.

That evening as I waited for you to arrive home, significant errors continued. My crestfallen alter-ego spoke about a solipsistic, not a hedonistic frame of thinking. When you unlocked the door, you stripped off your blouse and called me a child playing out Freud's infantile regression. Your pouting pink nipples held me, and I wanted some logical mode to stop misleading myself that you even existed. We were having sex. Your mouth between my legs when I realized you are not who you thought you were, and neither was I. In fact, we had become either Aquinas and Agrippina or Burroughs and Hypatia.

Mahalo's from Cicero began to arrive, but Father Damien intercepted them and suspected me for Queen Liliuokalani's death. Polynesian gladiatorial guards stormed in. I was taken to a palace where my existence was denied, leaving me to ponder whether my indifference to myself is a state of mind or am I a minor character alluded too in Treasure Island.

When the self-loathing peaked, my chest was ripped open, a needle was pushed into my heart, blood was perfusing through tubes into a trough where honeycreeper birds feasted. Crimson colors circled my thoughts, there you were, sitting on a barstool, drink in hand. You pointed a finger, yelling, as usual, telling all you never liked the texture of me. You preferred your lovers to have physical strength, not strength of character. Who wants to be with someone who thinks instead of one that feels, who reacts with intensity without pondering. With tears in my eyes from the rejection, I left to resuscitate the sad-faced animals going 'round on a carousel. Realizing my heart was insignificant compared to my brain, they asked the music to be changed to Hawaiian ballads. The giraffe recited stories from Tales of the South Pacific while a lion impersonated Captain Cook. Afterward, I was brought to a ridge overlooking the ocean by the police. I was questioned by transient humpback whales, who found me unfit to be called insane.

I recall the day we sought redemption. We had just returned from watching the sunrise from Haleakala. We realized everything about us was random and sometimes cruel. There was a note on the coffee table, our dog could not take living with us anymore. She said the apartment either smelled of lust or combustive misery. Anyway, she felt like a Siamese cat trapped in the body of a dachshund, she was off to Bangkok for a species change.

The last patron saint of discontent knew the world was terrible. Jung had become a photographer sharing quarters with Strindberg, who identifies himself as Louis Armstrong and Nijinsky, who wandered the streets at night in search of himself. In an awful nightmare, they all experienced the Dance of Death on the border of *der Genius,* and *whatever remains, however, improbable must be the truth.* I yearned to be there. I no longer believed in wholeness or possessions. I saw a world acting on impulse. I insisted on entering the mind of God and unimpressed, I replaced the delusion of words with a poet's flair for the unimaginable. Angry troops immediately marched into my head and carted me to a musical performance of my own demise.

You were in the kitchen, rethinking Hon Chew Hee's paintings. Colors from the inside of Kona winds filled your thoughts. We were past rejecting social norms, any norms, in fact. Pavarotti was singing Nessum Dorma while a coven of punchbowl schizophrenics sang Hawaiian wedding songs. The sounds of birds, ocean, and music perfectly blended because none of this existed except for the audience who were Vietnam Veterans who were being lied too about their existence.

I fell to my knees, when you lifted your sarong, your vagina was oblong and your thoughts black. I looked for my reasons, I searched my mind for explanations about reconciliation, but they rapidly disintegrated, and only paradoxes remained. I ripped at your flesh, filling the gap between cerebral and visceral with images of surfboard artwork, something Elvis could paint, but the Beamer's would despise. The reflection in the mirror with a smug, indulgent attitude put it succinctly: punishment is always oversimplified.

I escaped from Diamond Head again. The polyester Hawaiian shirt gangs were on my trail, and from the side road, I stumbled into my tortured mind's furthest dungeon. Where your words obliterated whatever it was I dreamed about that would raise intellectual verse to unforgivable ecstasy. You said I had the concerns of a genius, but I lacked the courage to grieve for my sanity. The compass you gave me before having sex with the neighborhood showed the effects of imitation. Nothing is real when imagination is a branding iron that your mind craves.

All things are more significant than themselves, that is only true when you have little enthusiasm for what you have become. My legs are my pallbearers. When you said good-bye, why didn't you serve me poison sashimi? Then I could have debated with the angels instead of that existential waitress with huge sunburned breasts you accused me of sleeping with.

My fingers wanted to find that slit you continually demanded, I lick. I needed to see my blood cover the walls in that little grass shack, that record you played over and over. Chuckling at me for not caring, enlightenment struck you. I was to be the next character introduced in the novel you never completed. A cross between Gatsby and Ulysses.

With a choice of birth, rebirth, or demise, the truth unravels and becomes utterly fearless. I will always be an unpredictable continuum and never at rest to give you what you anticipated. I am me, a vicious shark in the confines of a small mind. I am either going mad or returning from madness. My aspirations are as delicate as Hawaiian rainbows, but you, with your bitter sarcasm, belong in a script by Tennessee Williams.

Being Dead is Comfortable until you Die

Many of us are dead,
dead, and forgotten to ourselves.
It takes no time to die,
you wake up, hate yourself,
have coffee and leave for work.

On the way, you slit your wrists,
once there, you shoot yourself in the temple.
For lunch, you jump from the roof.
When it is time to leave, you drive to the ocean.
In the bar you frequent, a friend strangles you.
Instead of playing the jukebox
you put your head through it.
Outside, a train finds you.

Once home,
the kids pelt you with rocks,
while your wife serves you poisoned food,

Television reinforces your death,
questioning your sanity.
In the yard, dogs attack
while vultures wait their turn.
There is no light in the darkness, and darkness fills in the day.

I was born on the coldest day of the year.
The windows were cracked and caked with ice.
The air was acrid from the events taking place in the next bed.
Somebody had died, a man with a mortgage,
the man had been fed pills 'til his wallet was empty.
When the priest arrived, the doctor told him,
"Being dead is comfortable until you die."
Now, I would replace that person.

The holiday procession heads for a tavern,
I am too busy dying to join.
My lover demands the money she has earned.

I give her my best, but she loathes me more than I
despise myself.
On the way to nowhere, the road opens,
I am swallowed up by nothing,
nothing at all
just my thoughts.

The End

I did not pick the day, though a partial rainbow could be seen.
I went the distance, arriving as the rainbow was dissipating.
I searched for what I had spent a lifetime trying to achieve,
yet, all I could find was the end.
The end.

I turned in all directions, anticipating a mind full of beauty,
but consequences
entwine to form a pattern.
Without a place to run, continuing did not exist.
I thought I had shelved myself
and had become who I perceived,
but this was untrue.

There were reflections from mirrors,

none were satisfying.
Unquenchable,
this desire to continue became absolute,
but the end is deafening in its enlightenment.
I had expected full rainbows and dreams illuminated,
then in an instant, I understood.
Hope was a frayed rope unraveling
and laughter, as sharp as any dagger.

There were voices, speaking in rhythms.
I offered them my ambitions,
they wanted the opposite of what I could provide.
In all directions one day was leaping to the next
becoming a remembrance of nothing scholarly.
Indifference is a thief that takes nothing,
a menace we frighten ourselves with against
the tributes, we want to garner.

There are no doors, no windows, no words poetic,
just an oblique shadow
revealing the curvature of limitation.

I am in the same place, I have always been
but now, at the end,
I have no self-interest.

BIOGRAPHY

Philip M. Butera grew up in Buffalo, NY, earned a BS degree From Gannon College in Erie, PA, served in the US Navy then received an MA in Psychology from Simon Fraser University in Vancouver, Canada. He has published two books of poetry, "Mirror Images and Shards of Glass" and "Dark Images at Sea." His first novel, "Caught Between," a crime novel will be available in Summer 2020. He is completing his second novel, "Far from Here," a domestic thriller about love going terribly awry. His poetry appears in Journals and Magazines. He was a contributing editor for EatSleepWrite.net 2016-17 and a column in the quarterly magazine, Per Niente, 2016-2018. Philip won full scholarships to the 2017 Palm Beach Poetry Festival, 2017 Creative Capital Workshops, and Creative Capital Advanced Weekend Workshop 2018. The Cultural Council of Palm Beach County premiered his play, "The Apparition," and exhibited his poetry from February to March 2019. The Artists Guild Gallery/Boca Raton Museum of Art presented, "The Apparition" in December 2019. He has participated in the Arts Mentoring program developed by the Florida Department of State, Division of Cultural Affairs. Philip is the publicity coordinator for Mystery Writers of America - Florida Chapter, Sleuthfest 2018-2020. He lives in Boynton Beach, Florida.

CPSIA information can be obtained
at www.ICGtesting.com
Printed in the USA
JSHW010304100520
5506JS00004B/80

9 781946 675378